For The Lovers &
The Broken Hearted

Dalec Cromwell

BookLeaf Publishing

India | USA | UK

Presentation by *BookLeaf Publishing*

Web: www.bookleafpub.com

E-mail: info@bookleafpub.com

ISBN: 9789357696128

First edition 2023

*Andrea. Dalen. Isaiah. Maysun. Nolen.
Oaklyn. Ramé. Sadé. Taméa. Tim.*

With love, this is for you all.

ACKNOWLEDGEMENT

Becky. Moriah. Kate. Sonovia. Zeena.

Thank you ladies!

PREFACE

Embarked on a journey religiously, and internally over this past year. I lost and gain a lot along the road. I realized most things in life aren't for the long term but for the lessons learned.

A Beautiful Tragedy

What a conundrum, "A Beautiful tragedy"
I guess this is when lies and deceit
Suppose to turn you into a vicious beast
Cursing everything you see
But instead you became a gentle gem
With so much peace, love, and life burning
within

Fireflies

Closed eyed
Darken skies
I dreamt of the nights
Spent catching fireflies
Bottle inside
They'd illuminate
Odd how something so small
Could lighten the dark
Like what her smile
Did to my heart

Spare The Satisfaction

Broken pieces
Lay out on the floor
Hold keep
As she walks out the door
Last thing I want her to see
Is the gathering of shattering
Pieces of me

Avon

Mouth full of lies
To my surprise
She was a wolf, in sheep's disguise

For The Love of The Sea

Waves to the shore
She was violent
She was beautiful
Many admired
Her chaotic grace,
From afar.
I of the brazen few
Dove beneath her sea
Her allure was paralyzing
Her depth kissed my lips
I sang her blues.
I

D
R
O
W
N
E
D.

Untitled

I saw the forest in her eyes
I walked deeper and deeper
Her tears made them greener
Sunshine in her smile
Masked my darken clouds.

Distant Lover

I ask "will you miss me while I'm gone?"

She says, "I miss you while you're here.
The truth is in your eyes.
I can feel the distance in your stare."

The Dark Side of Love

I tried to drown my demons,
In this bottle of sin.
They only learned to swim.
So I befriended them.

Whole Hearted

Emotional security was never the question.
Like lack of leadership was what's got you
stressing?
Airing out dirty laundry, that is just
embarrassing.
Three of his children is what you are possessing.
But leadership caused your digression?
Accountability.
Communication.
Insecurities.
Trustworthiness.

Cause this separation.
Too much to be honest with the mirror.
So you take to social media.
To watch the back-patters appear.
Fuck a message.
Here's an idea!
Speak truth to the mirror it makes those demons
disappear.

Untitled

The fear in trust
The scare of faith in another
Emotional rollercoaster
Has me questioning my lover

Trauma Hearted

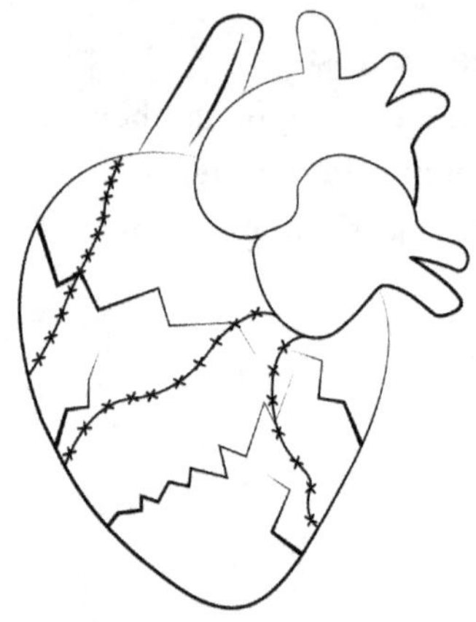

You rather be the treacherous truth or a lovely
lie?
Truth be told in a blink of an eye
Truth of this lie
Would kill what's between you and I
Love does not reside here, inside
Broken-hearted or cold-hearted?
Chose your poison
Whichever, caused this to end
So to my former dearly beloved
My now dearly departed
You're just another victim
Of the trauma hearted

Donielle

You said to write about us
I was never really sure what to write
But here I am tonight
With the thoughts I couldn't put to pad
When you'd ask.
A free mind with a blacken heart
Carrying regrets from when we last fought
I came to the conclusion it was no one's fault,
The short time we spent
Was such a beautiful waltz.
You said
"I'll read what you write, when it's about us."
So this is solely for you
Sorry for the delay.
Just hope this reaches you before it's too late.

Sky is Crying

The sky is crying
As walk down the street
The rain hides
Tears in my eyes
The sky is crying
And the tears run down my cheek
The sky is crying
And I'm dying
Just to hear her speak

Untitled

In this past year
I learned to find beauty in the tears
These eyes have masked many storms
Left my heart and soul torn
A living purgatory
Joy and pain use my flesh as a dormitory
In a life of sin
Will I win in the end?
I lost one
Before I birthed a son
Watched innocence be taken on the run
Dreams that the worse has yet to come
I've seen truths flee
As deceit takes her seat
Life of retaliation
Led to litigation
Take the good with the bad
Smile with the sad
Much beauty in the shades of gray
Alhamdulillah for they are only here to stay.

Lover's Conversation

She says, "the eyes are the windows to your soul. I've noticed there is so much rain on your windowpane."

My reply, "cause inside is a hurricane. Would you go if I showed you the pain?"
She states, "of course, I will stay."

To which I simply say, "The rain you see is the tears that can longer fall. They cloud my eyes, blur my vision, block my intuition. Trauma has caused me not to make the best decisions. I travel through women, you could be the next victim."

Using her best wisdom, she stayed and prayed for my trauma of abandonment she felt her love could bandage it.

Woman Of My Dreams

I met her at a coffee shop
Her smile made my heart stop
She was breathtaking
With a captivating conversation
As I hung onto her every word
Minutes turned into hours
This may sound absurd
Her every "I" was replaced with "our"
This feeling was so new to me
But knew I didn't want to spend the rest of this
life without her

ROI

Return on your interest
Return on your instincts
Return on your inferences
Return on your interactions
Return on your initiative
Return on your ideals
Return on your intimacy
Return on your influence
Return on your intelligence
Return on your intellect
Return on your intentions…
For the lovers and the broken heart
Value the return on your investments
For it is the thin line between each of us.

Anomaly Of Love

We tend to ignore the red flags
Thoughts of "oh that's just a character anomaly"
Until the "character anomaly" becomes
challenging
It is then when we realize, character red flags
"Character anomaly" does not exist
Just the anomaly of love
This is why love is so hard to find

Small Wins

Celebrate the little victories
For they strengthen your will
Broaden your smile
Lighten your heart
Warm your soul
Celebrate the little victories
For they weaken your enemies

Word to Live By

It ain't always about the story.
But the journey.
There is so much more beauty in the journey.
Than in the story.
Focus on your journey.
Shit the story would tell itself.

For The Lovers & The Broken-Hearted

For the lovers & the broken-hearted
No matter how light or darken
Your journey has gotten
Keep walking.